Copyright © 2022 Rachel Beckles
All rights reserved. No portion of this book may be reproduced in any form without permission from the publisher, except as permitted by U.K. copyright law. For permissions contact:
info@RachelBeckles.com

Welcome!

This workbook will help you to plan a book for your business in no time. There are simple steps to follow with space to make all of your notes. Once you have finished, use your phone to take a picture of your handwritten notes and press 'copy text' or download a text scanner and your notes will be typed up in an instant!

WWW.RACHELBECKLES.COM   @RACHELBECKLES

Remember!

'You are 42% more likely to accomplish your goals if you write them down''

MARIE FORLEO

MY INTENTIONS

What would you like this book to do for your business?

- Help you to get paid speaking engagements
- Entice new customers/clients as a gift
- Be an additional source of income
- Be used as a free lead magnet to grow your mailing list
- Aid you in facilitating workshops

I would like my book to help me to:
_____
_____
_____
_____
_____
_____
_____
_____

Be specific!

RACHEL BECKLES ✦ **Workbook**

CHECKLIST

		YES	NO
1	Set clear intentions for your book. It's ok if this book is just an experiment and you are trying something new.	☐	☐
2	Find at least two non-fiction books you like and make note of your likes and dislikes about them - success leaves clues!	☐	☐
3	Write down how you want your audience to feel after they have read your book and why. Are there any actions you would like them to take? Think about products and services you provide that you could direct them to.	☐	☐
4	Give yourself permission to be a newbie author and be kind to yourself.	☐	☐

NOTE TAKING

How do you take notes?
Think about how you record and retain information best.

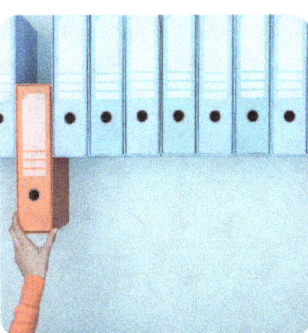

Remember

You can use more than one method but be careful not to confuse yourself and double your workload.

Synchronise your online documents with apps on your phone so you can work on the go.

If you have physical notes, keep them in the same place at home so you always know where to find them.

RACHEL BECKLES ★ WORKBOOK

CHECKLIST

		YES	NO
1	Explore your favourite way to take notes, try a few ways.	☐	☐
2	A huge brain dump of all of your ideas/potential subject matter for your book.	☐	☐
3	Make a note of any books that you would like to reference.	☐	☐
4	Collate old notes you have written about your area of knowledge.	☐	☐
5	Write down what you would like your book to include.	☐	☐

TITLE IDEAS

To create a simple and effective title think of::

1.	A skill that your audience would like to develop/ A pain point that your customers/audience have/ A goal that they would like to achieve
2.	A number of steps that this goal is going to take to achieve
3.	A realistic measure of time based on your audience (think about their age, experience, skillset, free time, budget)

Remember!

Use key words that your audience will google/type in on social media or search engine.

TITLE IDEAS

- ✓ 10 tips to...

- ✓ Learn how to _ in _ easy steps

- ✓ Improve your _ in _ minutes

- ✓ A beginners guide to _

- ✓ How to _ in _ steps

Potential titles

_____
_____
_____
_____
_____

RACHEL BECKLES ★ WORKBOOK

CHECKLIST

		YES	NO
1	Decide on a title/working title for your book.	☐	☐
2	Share your book title idea with your audience/existing customers.	☐	☐
3	Start collecting email addresses from people who are interested in your book to keep them informed of its progress.	☐	☐

COVER DESIGN

Can you design your book yourself or do you need help?

	I have the skill to do it myself	I want to hire help
Platform (examples but there are many more!)	Canva Adobe InDesign Picmonkey	Upwork Fiverr Guru Linkedin Instagram
Research	Test out a few programs to find the one that supports your budget, computer and skillset	Ask designers about their availability, get quotes, talk to them (this is a great way to find out about their communication skills, temperament and their understanding of your project)
Don't forget	If you are new to the program you choose, please remember it takes time to learn how to use them	Make sure the freelancer is aware of; • Your timeframe • The format/size of book • If its a paperback they will ask the page count (to design the cover the right size)
Potential questions to ask	Are there any pre-made templates that I can adapt for my cover?	What will the timeframe be? Will I have to pay for any revisions? Would you be willing to sign a contract to proetect my front cover?

RACHEL BECKLES ★ **WORKBOOK**

How will doing this first, help?

- This part can take longer than you think!
- You can promote you book
- 7 touch theory
- Attract new customers
- Get excited!!!

It is so much easier to get your audience excited about something they can **see** and potentially own.

Did you know you can pre-sell a book based on the front cover?

Remember!

Look at existing book covers in your niche.
Our aim is to create a cover that stands out but can be identified quickly.

We don't have to be an expert in cover design, we just need to know what works well and to take inspiration from it.

Bare in mind most people will see your cover at the size of your thumbnail on their phone!

CHECKLIST

		YES	NO
1	Decide if you are going to create your own cover or hire help.	☐	☐
2	Look at existing book covers in that niche - look for design similarities you would like to include.	☐	☐
3	Have you thought about ways that your cover can stand out amongst books within your niche?	☐	☐
4	Have you created two or three covers and let your audience vote for their favourite?	☐	☐

RACHEL BECKLES ★ **WORKBOOK**

Email Marketing

Email your audience and let them know that you have a new book coming out soon! You don't have to give them a date of publication at this point. If you don't have a mailing system or a way of contacting your customers in bulk, now is the time to start one up.

Why?
- Send your audience shoppable landing pages/links/websites
- Connect and stay in touch with your new audience
- Free marketing
- Organic audience who have already shown interest in your business
- Easy to measure engagement using email services link Mailchimp
- Keeps your audience in touch with your new products
- You own your mailing list!
- Lower conversion rate

Email is king of marketing!

You can literally use a spreadsheet or a word document to get you started. Your email list is something that you will ALWAYS own. It is a direct connection between you and your audience. Social media platforms die and crash but your mailing list goes with you wherever you like! With your mailing list you can directly market new services and products directly to your customers.

GDPR

GDPR - (general data protection regulation) in the UK and Europe means as businesses we are sensitive to the rights of individuals with regard to their personal data.
Please do not add people to your mailing lists without their permission. Make sure people have the ability to unsubscribe at anytime. For more information, please visit

www.gov.uk/data-protection

CHECKLIST

		YES	NO
1	Decide on your mailing list service - even if it's just a spreadsheet!	☐	☐
2	Collate all solicited email addresses you have been given (GDPR).	☐	☐
3	Write an email about your upcoming book and send it to your mailing list!	☐	☐
4	If you have an existing website, create an email field to capture on your website.	☐	☐

RACHEL BECKLES　　　　　　　　　　WORKBOOK

NOTES SPACE

RACHEL BECKLES ★ WORKBOOK

Remember!

When you have collected email addresses, ask them if they would like an exclusive look at your book when it's finished (we will use them as early readers later)

COPYRIGHT

Copyright protects your work and stops others from using it without your permission.

You get copyright protection automatically - you don't have to apply or pay a fee. There isn't a register of copyright works in the UK.

You automatically get copyright protection when you create:

- original literary, dramatic, musical and artistic work, including illustration and photography
- original non-literary written work, such as software, web content and databases
- sound and music recordings
- film and television recordings
- broadcasts
- the layout of published editions of written, dramatic and musical works
- You can mark your work with the copyright symbol (©), your name and the year of creation. Whether you mark the work or not doesn't affect the level of protection you have.

www.gov.uk (June2022)

Remember!

Write a copyright disclaimer for your book and save it (copyright done!)
There are lots of templates you can google and adapt

COPYRIGHT

There are many companies that will be able to support you with copyright. One used by many authors in the UK is Copyright house.

Remember!

With any additional copyright protection, you choose, please read their terms and conditions to ensure you retain all of the rights of your work.

Disclaimer

I am not a lawyer, please be sure to do your own additional research to ensure you feel comfortable with copyright law.

CHECKLIST

		YES	NO
1	Write a copyright disclaimer for your book and save it.	☐	☐
2	Carry out research around copyright law.	☐	☐
2	If you would like additional copyright protection chose company and read their terms and conditions to ensure you are not somehow signing the rights over to them!	☐	☐

PLAN YOUR BOOK

From your previous notes and the title you have decided on, brainstorm everything you want to include in this book.

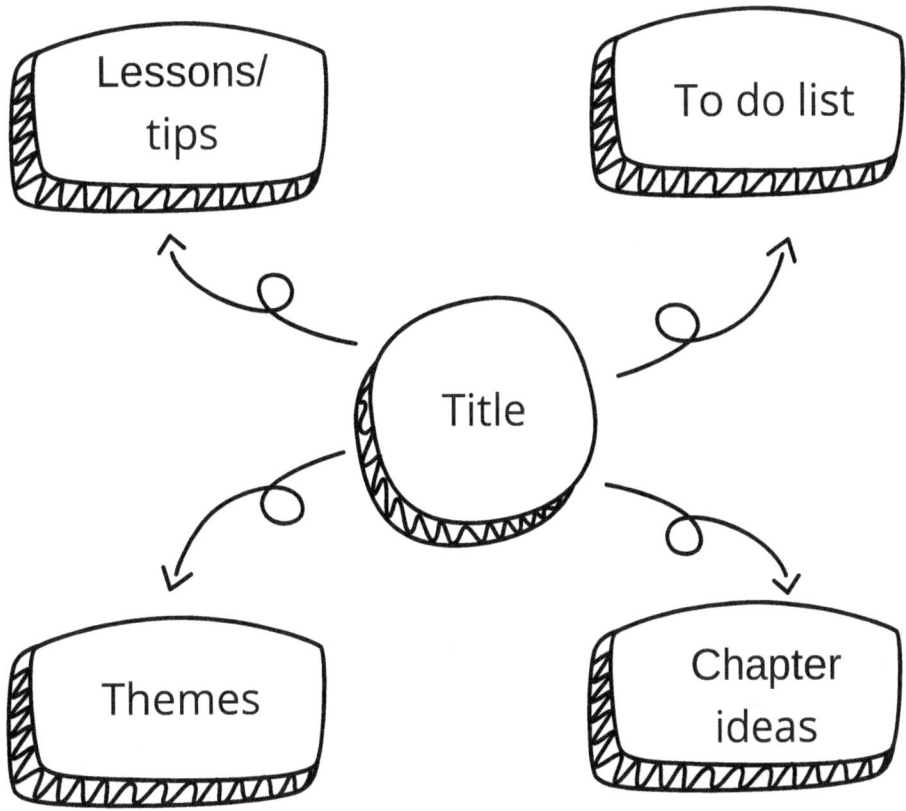

NOTES SPACE

KEEP ALL OF THESE NOTES!!

RACHEL BECKLES — WORKBOOK

'IF IN DOUBT THINK W.W.S.D'

'Want, work, stop doing' - Sunny Lenarduzzi

What do you think that your customers <u>want</u> to know?

What <u>work</u> will your customers have to do to achieve this?

What will your customer need to have to <u>stop doing</u> to achieve their goal?

Remember!

You are writing a book that focuses on:
- Skills that your audience would like to develop
- Pain points that they have
- Goals that they would like to achieve

CHECKLIST

		YES	NO
1	Write all of your ideas down based on the title of your book.	☐	☐
2	Find a common theme/highlight a particular topic or niche that can be used to create chapters.	☐	☐
3	Research reputable people/organisations that support and reiterate your ideas.	☐	☐

RACHEL BECKLES — WORKBOOK

CHAPTER OUTLINES

Plan the points that you would like to make in each chapter.

CHAPTER ONE	

CHAPTER TWO	

CHAPTER THREE	

CHAPTER FOUR	

CHAPTER FIVE	

CHAPTER SIX	

RACHEL BECKLES — *WORKBOOK*

CHAPTER OUTLINES

CHAPTER SEVEN	

CHAPTER EIGHT	

CHAPTER NINE	

CHAPTER TEN	

BONUS CHAPTER	

BONUS CONENT	

CHAPTER STRUCTIRE

Point
(e.g. a tip, mistakes frequently made, a suggestion)

Use short simple sentences.
Consider adding a glossary to introduce new language.
Choose dynamic words that empower the reader.

↓

Research
(information from reputable sources)

Consider siting sources such as doctors, legal professionals, guidelines applicable to cities/countries.

↓

Advice
(lessons that you have learned from your experience)

This is where you can offer advice, suggestions and inform the reader of your products/services.

Make a list of references for your bibliography!

You can't edit a blank page so write as much down as you can.

Focus on creating a book that you would like to receive or buy if you were new to your business.

Over deliver on 'why' advice or information, your clients will respect and value your opinion more and will be more likely to recommend your book to their friends. This way you can also upsell your 'how' through your products, services or content at a later date.

If you are designing the book yourself you might want to design as you write - look at templates available that can be used for commercial use.

Don't over complicate the language - remember you are an expert, readers will disengage - create a glossary if you are introducing your reader to new vocabulary.

Save any notes that you make, they may come in handy for another book/free giveaway later on!

Write in short or long burst whatever works for you.

Expand on each point that you have made in the grid you prepared.

PLAN - CHAPTER 1

PLAN - CHAPTER 2

PLAN - CHAPTER 3

PLAN - CHAPTER 4

PLAN - CHAPTER 5

PLAN - CHAPTER 6

PLAN - CHAPTER 7

PLAN - CHAPTER 8

PLAN - CHAPTER 9

PLAN - CHAPTER 10

EDIT YOUR BOOK

Tools you can use to help

You can also hire an editor on platforms such as:
- Fiverr
- Guru
- People per hour
- LinkedIn

CHECKLIST

		YES	NO

1. Plan chapter ideas for your book. Any bonus content you create can be used for freebies/social media.

2. Draft out each chapter remembering the structure **Point - research - advice.**

3. Make a list of references for your bibliography.

4. Ask your audience what they would like to read about.

5. Create a glossary for any words related to your specific area that your readers may be unfamiliar with.

6. Use software, an application or an online tool for an initial edit of the first draft of the book.

RACHEL BECKLES — WORKBOOK

PRE- ORDERS

Remember

- Upsell your product tomake sure you are in profit at the end of your launch
- Calculate shipping costs and factor it into your pre-order price

What will you offer?

- Signed copies?
- Additional freebies?
- NFTs?
- Discounts codes?

EMAIL PLATFORMS TO EXPLORE

If you don't have a website , you could create a pre-order offer using one of the websites below.

SELLING ADVERTISING AT THE BACK OF YOUR BOOK

Contact local businesses related to, but not directly competing with yours and offer them an advert space at the back of your book.

For example, if you are an estate agent writing a guide about property in a particular area, you could contact:

- local cleaners
- plumbers
- gardeners
- waste collection services

Offer the company copies of the book that they can give away for free or sell to their customers.

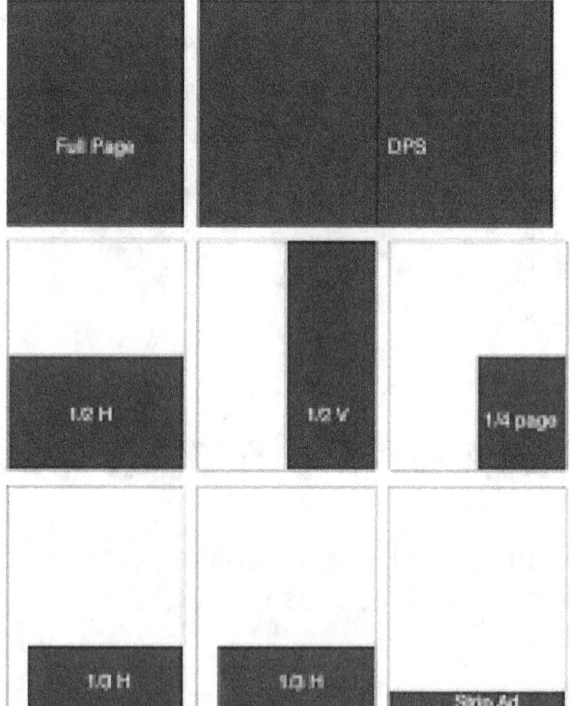

Remember to price the offer so you are still in profit after you give the free copies

RACHEL BECKLES **WORKBOOK**

Pitch them your book

Here is a pitch I might receive as a self-publishing coach:

Dear Rachel

My name is Elmo and I am a printer based in South London. I enjoy watching your Instagram page and found the reel about how to get back into your writing really helpful!
I am writing a book called 10 tips to formatting your book, would you like an exclusive read? I often get asked about self publishing support and wondered if you would be interested in the advertising space I have available at the back of my book.
In addition to the following offers, if you would like to order more copies of the book, I can offer them do you at a wholesale price.

I look forward to hearing from you.
Kindest regards

Elmo

Remember!

- Address the business owner by name whenever possible
- Personalise the message (no cut and paste)
- Remember to price the offer so you are still in profit after you give the free copies

CHECKLIST

		YES	NO
1	Decide on a pre-order strategy.	☐	☐
2	Set a launch date.	☐	☐
3	Set a target of how many adverts I want to sell at the back of your book.	☐	☐
4	Find companies that might be interested in buying advertising space at the back of my book.	☐	☐

Early readers

Ask your mailing list if they would like to get an exclusive look at your book. You can also ask loyal followers, customers, friends and family to help you.

Consider offering them a gift to thank them for their help.

- Discount vouchers
- A free copy of the book
- A free product

Create a survey

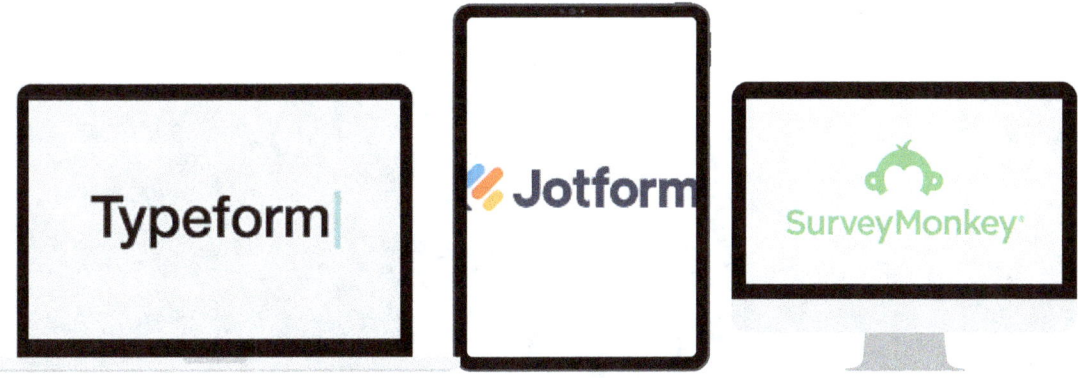

Give your early readers a set time to read the book and respond to the questionnaire. Consider asking questions like;

- What was your favourite piece of information?
- Was there anything you didn't understand?
- Was there anything you didn't enjoy reading?
- Do you think there was anything missing?

CHECKLIST

		YES	NO
1	Use the feedback to complete draft number two.	☐	☐
2	Proofread or hire proof reader.	☐	☐
3	Share your progress with your audience - early readers.	☐	☐

RACHEL BECKLES ✶ WORKBOOK

Printing styles

Printing style	Pros	Cons
Batch printing	<ul><li>Great for low-cost printing</li><li>Better quality paper</li></ul>	<ul><li>Expensive upfront costs</li><li>Boxes everywhere!</li><li>Slow return on investment</li><li>If you find a mistake, you will end up with lots of poor quality stock - eek!</li></ul>
Print on demand (P.O.D) Platforms	<ul><li>Little/No upfront costs</li><li>Delivered to the customer worldwide*</li><li>You can order small numbers of your book</li></ul>	<ul><li>Not all sized books are printed worldwide</li><li>You can only print in black and white or colour</li></ul>
Ebooks	<ul><li>No paper required!</li><li>Offer free books to your audience</li><li>Worldwide distribution</li></ul>	Don't have that new book smell!

*Distribution does not include Cuba, Iran, North Korea, Sudan and Syria. Please visited the Amazon website for further information on shipping restrictions

RACHEL BECKLES ★ WORKBOOK

Amazon KDP

KDP will allow you do produce paperback (page min number 24, hardback (min number of pages 75) and ebooks. You will need;

- ✓ Your IBAN number from your bank statement

- ✓ A unique taxpayer reference (UTR) or your National Insurance Number

- ✓ An ISBN (you can get a free one from Amazon) or purchase one from https://www.nielsenisbnstore.com

- ✓ A PDF copy of your front and back cover with your front cover on the right and your back cover on the left

- ✓ A PDF of the interior of your book

Other P.O.D platforms
Print On Demand

Other eBook platforms

- ✓ Applebooks
- ✓ Google play
- ✓ Kobo
- ✓ Smashwords
- ✓ Draft2Digital

Ebook creators

Help you to ensure the layout of your book stays in the same configuration on all devices.

ISBN

The International Standard Book Number (ISBN) is a way of identifying an individual book.

- Neilson.com - you can buy single ISBN numbers or bundles
- Free from Amazon

Do I need ISBN?

- They help to track sales (for ranking purposes)
- Make the books easy to scan in shops
- Not required for a book that you intend to give away for free
- They are not required for ebooks
- Can be assigned for free from Amazon KPD

CHECKLIST

		YES	NO
1	Chose a platform to publish your book.	☐	☐
2	Create a PDF of your interior for your paperback book	☐	☐
3	Create a PDF of your front(and back) cover. (The front should be on the left and the back on the right)	☐	☐
4	Print a sample copy of your book and get feedback from friends and family.	☐	☐
5	Use a program such as Kindle Create to create an eBook format of your book (EPUB, DOCX, KPF).	☐	☐
6	Ensure that you have resized (or your freelancer has created) the cover to create an ebook cover.	☐	☐

Social Media

Tips

- Pick two platforms- master them! Learn how to share posts, interpret analytics and grow your following with confidence
- Use one platform to help you to promote and grow another
- Consider using a scheduling app like 'Later' to help you create a regular content strategy
- Look at your analytics regularly to ensure that you are getting the most from each post
- Don't forget to be social!

How will they help?

- Expand your reach outside your network
- Increase your views
- Build community awareness
- Follow and take part in conversations about your subject to create organic traffic. Like and comment on relevant posts to make yourself visible to potential customers
- Allow you to be discovered in relevant #

Remember!

Email is king! Social media is not a secure method of contact. If a platform goes down we can lose hundreds of contacts. This is why our mailing list is vital we have the ability to contact our customers via email so keep collecting addresses.

Instagram

Pros →

- Very visual platform
- You can use hashtags to search and be discovered
- 30 million UK users
- 1 billion worldwide users

Cons →

- Timing of posts is key
- Easy to fall low in the algorithm if you don't use it regularly

Remember to;

- Keep your stories active to stay in people's minds
- Engage (DMs, comments, interact with stories)
- Create stories that your audience can interact with using polls and questions
- Use a selection of hashtags
- Create carousels (multiple pictures/clips in one post that people swipe through) for longer engagement
- Add captions to your videos
- Flag warm leads
- Try out Reels!

INSTAGRAM CHECKLIST

                                                                                       YES   NO

1. Is your account a business account?

2. Are you using your insights to post content that gets the highest engagement from your followers?

3. Is your Bio clear about who you are and what you do?

4. Do people know where you are?

5. Do you post regular content?

6. Do you post a combination of reels, pictures and stories?

7. Have you ever gone 'live' on your own or with a happy customer?

RACHEL BECKLES   ✶   WORKBOOK

Facebook messenger

Pros →

- Direct marketing to warm leads
- Opportunity to build relationships with your audience

Cons →

- I just don't like it much!
- Tries to get up in your business!

Remember to;

- Remain professional when you send anyone a direct message (DM)
- Create groups in which like-minded people can interact in
- Share links to all of your products and services

FACEBOOK MESSENGER CHECKLIST

                                                                          YES   NO

1 Are you sending direct messages to your existing customers to engage and get reviews?

2 Are you connecting with local shops who could potentially buy your books wholesale?

3 Are you interacting with any message groups?

RACHEL BECKLES   WORKBOOK

LinkedIn

Pros →

- Great networking/job opportunities
- More authority credibility than other platforms
- Improve your search engine rank (SEO)
- 31 million UK users
- 660 million users worldwide

Cons →

- Potential spammy sites contacting you
- Expensive if you choose to use additional services

Remember to;

- Make your profile public
- Update your location
- Update your profile picture, background and URL
- Update your headline
- Request testimonials

LINKEDIN CHECKLIST

                                                                                                    YES   NO

1. Do you have up-to-date contact details available?

2. Is your profile showcasing your most recent work?

3. Is there a photo of you on your profile?

4. Have you used relevant keywords in your profile?

Tiktok

Pros →

- Relatively new platform
- Different algorithm - easy to be discovered
- #Booktok is huge!

Cons →

- Massively addictive - time thief!!
- Can be time-consuming to create videos
- Fiddly to get used to

Remember to;

- Make your profile public
- Update your bio
- Use trending sounds/video formats relevant to your genre
- Save your drafts on your phone/screen record videos to use on Instagram/Facebook etc
- Consider doing duet videos to engage a new audience

TIKTOK CHECKLIST

                                                          YES   NO

1   Are you using hashtags that are relevant to
    your field?

2   Have you recorded posts sharing quick tips for
    potential customers?

3   Are you recreating any current trends, keeping
    the content about your field?

4   Encouraging your Tiktok follows to find you on
    another platform to see a different style of
    content?

Please Remember

- Social media is a tool **NOT** an obligation.
- Each platform is designed to keep you on there as long as possible - don't let them overwhelm you.
- The advice about social media **ALWAYS** says post more - do what you can to maintain consistency e.g twice a week.
- Pick your favourite platform - one is plenty - two are great.

Celebrate Your Launch!

You are amazing make sure you celebrate!

What will your launch look like?

- Will you have a book launch?
- Will it be virtual, at your business or in a hired venue?
- What other businesses can you collaborate with to make it more exciting?

CHECKLIST

		YES	NO

1. Decide on a weekly social media post strategy.

2. Use the bonus chapter ideas to create posts/videos for social media.

3. Ensure the bios are up to date on each platform with links to websites or products.

4. Plan your book launch! Invite everyone to share photos on their social media.

5. Think of offers, raffles and giveaways you can share during your launch.

6. Collect email addresses of those who attend your launch to grow your mailing list.

7. Use the photos from your launch for additional social media content!

Ideas For Expansion

What will you do next? Keep the momentum going! the best thing to promote your book is...another book!

Rinse and repeat this process using the notes that you made that didn't become part of your book.

Potential ideas for expansion

Products

- A journal specific to your niche
- A Colouring book
- A workbook
- Merchandise
- An audiobook

Services

- Speaking at events
- Workshops
- A course to sell on a platform like **Kujabi** or **Thinkific**
- A podcast (with the option of contributions from patron

Rachel's Final Thought

- Effortless doesn't exist this book wont write itself
- Take your time and enjoy the process - it will show in your book!
- Success leaves clues
- Done is better than perfect

That's all folks!

Thank you!

Have a great week and I look forward to catching up with you next video!

 Self-publishing with Rachel Beckles

 @rachelbeckles

THANK YOU!

I really look forward to hearing all about your book! When it's finished take a picture and tag me on Instagram I can't wait to see! @rachelbeckles

RACHELBECKLES.COM

YOUR BRAND NAME HERE
INSTRUCTOR

RACHEL BECKLES
Self-Publishing Addict

I always sign copies of one of my stories for children with;
'Life is an adventure, follow your dreams!'
Grown ups! The same applies to your too - just plan the journey x

RACHEL BECKLES'
CLIENT TESTIMONIALS

DOMINIQUE @BOOKS_OF_COLOUR

'I Just want to say thank you for content that you provided on the self-publishing course. It was great. I learned a lot and it has been really helpful. I have started to apply some of the things I have learnt and it was all very useful. It has helped me to see things as more achievable and put things into practice.'

GHOSTWRITING CLIENT

I am very happy with the story I got! I gave Rachel a very rough idea of what I wanted the story to be about. Rachel immediately understood what the story is about and brought the characters and ideas to life.

Right from the beginning of this project, I felt very involved in the process. Before writing the full story, Rachel sent me samples of different perspectives the story could be written in, this opened my mind to possibilities that I would not have explored myself. During the actual story, I am glad she felt free to write her own ideas and flexible enough for me to express my own ideas as she wrote each draft. Overall, I had a good experience using Rachel's service, and I look forward to using her service again in the future.

CASEY STYLES - @CASEYSTYLES

This course was super easy to follow considering I have never written a book before hand. Rachel's instructions were clear and precise which allowed me to complete it with ease. I highly recommend for 1st time Author's. I really loved how easy it was to access all the websites and all at affordable cost. But freeeeee is our favourite word now hehe. Thanks and good luck on your book.

NOTES SPACE

RACHEL BECKLES WORKBOOK

NOTES SPACE

RACHEL BECKLES ★ WORKBOOK

NOTES SPACE

NOTES SPACE

www.ingramcontent.com/pod-product-compliance
Lightning Source LLC
Chambersburg PA
CBHW080520220526
45465CB00006B/2542